Losing
a *Hero to*
Alzheimer's

The Story of Pearl

Patricia M. McClure

WESTBOW
PRESS®
A DIVISION OF THOMAS NELSON
& ZONDERVAN

WestBow Press books may be ordered through booksellers or by contacting:

WestBow Press
A Division of Thomas Nelson & Zondervan
1663 Liberty Drive
Bloomington, IN 47403
www.westbowpress.com
1 (866) 928-1240

ISBN: 978-1-5127-0721-2 (sc)
ISBN: 978-1-5127-0723-6 (hc)
ISBN: 978-1-5127-0722-9 (e)

Library of Congress Control Number: 2015912798

Print information available on the last page.

WestBow Press rev. date: 08/31/2015

I dedicate this book to my mother, the late Ann Shirley McClure (aka Pearl). You were truly a saint sent from the Lord. You helped shape me into the woman I am today. You were an awesome mother, friend, and confidant. You helped to change the world through your smile, your service, and the life that you lived. God allowed you to be my mother. I am forever grateful for every sacrifice you made for our family and me. Your living was not in vain, and your legacy will live on forever.

"I can't put a number to the years that I need you here on earth so I carry you with me daily in my heart."

—Patricia M. McClure

CONTENTS

PREFACE

*L*osing a Hero to Alzheimer's: The Story of Pearl has been in the making for the past ten years. I was waiting for the moment I was strong enough, emotionally and spiritually, to share my journey in caring for my mother with Alzheimer's. *Losing a Hero to Alzheimer's: The Story of Pearl* will show the epitome of a strong, spiritual woman who endured so much in her lifetime and positively impacted people's lives. Pearl was afflicted with the ugly disease of Alzheimer's, and her mental condition spiraled downward. As my mother's caregiver, I experienced a high level of stress and encountered many challenges. I will share some of Pearl's behavior and how they align with the cognitive declination stages according to the Alzheimer's Association.

I strongly acknowledge that it was only by the strength of God that I was able to endure this life-changing experience with a very limited support system. So many families are stricken by this disease on some level. I hope my story will give caregivers practical guidance who encounter this dreadful disease.

ACKNOWLEDGMENTS

I am so appreciative of my family and friends for believing in me. Thank you to my judicious editor, Chiquita R. Griffin. I want to thank my God-brother, Byron Barnes, for believing in me and listening to me whenever I wanted to talk about this book. I am grateful for my children who encouraged me while I wrote this book. Your continued interest and excitement is what kept me motivated. I want to give a special thanks to my husband (Pastor Eric H. Chessier) for standing by my side through thick and through thin. You treated my mother with love and patience, and for that I truly thank you.

INTRODUCTION

Ann Shirley Strayhon (aka Pearl) was born on December 26, 1934, in Chicago, Illinois. Raised in Hyde Park, she was the only girl of four children. Pearl met Jesse McClure while singing in the choir at a Baptist church on the South Side of Chicago. Jesse was from Little Rock, Arkansas. They later married, and to this union four children were born—three girls and one boy. I, Patricia Madina McClure, was the youngest daughter in the family.

Our family lived on the South Side of Chicago, and Pearl was our rock. She was a very spiritual woman and walked closely with God. By all accounts, Pearl was known for the love and kindness she showed her family, friends, and the community. She was a hands-on parent and active in her neighborhood.

After I, her youngest child, started school, Pearl began her career working at one of the largest skyscrapers in downtown Chicago. She was in a difficult marriage but found happiness in other outlets. She was also the full-time caregiver of one of her oldest brothers, who was handicapped.

Pearl did whatever she could to give her children various opportunities and experiences, which my father, Jesse, resented. He was bitter and selfish because he grew up with limited resources. Pearl's marital problems really started to take a toll on her, and she began showing signs of depression. In later years, she started to show early signs of Alzheimer's. Eventually, her coworkers started to see changes in her job performance. To avoid taking responsibility, some family members remained in denial that she had Alzheimer's. Pearl started to exhibit behaviors that jeopardized her safety and welfare which caused great concerns for me. It was also hard to accept that Pearl had a problem because she had always been so strong and independent.

Through this book I will do my best to illustrate the "characters" in my family and bring their personalities to life. This story is vey visual, dramatic, and emotionally driven, and you, the reader, will hopefully remain engaged from start to finish. My desire is that the reader will walk away with a practical understanding of the stages of Alzheimer's, and how this debilitating illness affects the family system.

CHAPTER 1

Mom's Early Days

My mother grew up on the South Side of Chicago, in Hyde Park, in the 1930s and 1940s. She was the youngest and the only girl of four children. Pearl was spoiled by her father, who died during her childhood. She was always unsure about his cause of death, and it was never discussed.

Pearl had three brothers: Patrick, Drew, and John, all in the US Army, although each in a different battalion. When they came home on leave, they doted on their little sister and would give her money before returning to military duty. Pearl talked about how her brothers sent her letters and sporadically called to check on her and "Maudie" (an affectionate nickname for Pearl's mom).

Maudie was a little different than most. Whispers among family members questioned if Maudie had a mental condition. Unfortunately, no one did anything to find out. According to Pearl, in those days, people just turned a blind eye and pretended everything was normal.

In her younger years, my mom always talked about her father and described him as a "neat and loving man." Pearl also shared how repugnantly Maudie treated her father. She said, "Mom wouldn't cook or clean the house even though she was at home all day." Maudie wasn't very affectionate, and she made very reprehensible, offensive comments to Pearl. She resented the fact that Pearl was "Daddy's little girl."

My mother never really talked about her mom during my childhood. Whenever Mom was asked questions about Maudie, she became evasive and changed the subject. It was apparent from Pearl's responses that she had some oppressive memories of her mom.

Still, as I got older, I began to ask more questions about my grandmother, and my mom reluctantly began to open up. I recall one time my mother's eyes welled with tears as she talked about her mother's senility and how her mother abused her. I felt terrible that my questions made her cry. One of my mother's favorite sayings was, "You should leave well enough alone," and from that day forward, I did just that. I stopped asking my mom about her mother. Some things remained a mystery to me. For example, I wondered if my grandmother ever worked or had any siblings.

Pearl described her mom as pretty and shared how she spoke eloquently, even though she could be categorized as eccentric and perhaps even weird. She shared a story about how Maudie once aggressively approached her and cut off her long, black, silky braids for no apparent reason. Sometimes Maudie accused Pearl of doing things just so she could justify spanking her. When I asked Mom why she didn't tell anyone about the abuse, she replied, "During that era, you dared not tell anybody!" Pearl knew at a very young age to behave because if she ever got into trouble, she wouldn't have any refuge. So she was careful never to do anything to draw attention to herself or her horrendously dysfunctional household.

Pearl came from an affluent family comprised of doctors, lawyers, judges, teachers, and other accomplished professionals. Her family members gave her money as a child to pay household bills and buy groceries for the home. Extended family members suspected something was wrong with Maudie's mind, which was why they helped out in any way they could. Pearl also suspected there was something wrong with her mother, but she had no one to talk to about it. Sometimes she had no clue about her mom whereabouts. Pearl wondered if anyone knew. As a result, Pearl went to stay with relatives in Waukegan and North Chicago on multiple occasions. Her extended family members were very nice to her, and when it was time to go back home to deal with her mom's bizarre behaviors, Pearl dreaded it. Maudie talked to herself and objects. She became angry when the objects didn't respond back. Maudie often got upset with Pearl for no apparent reason.

My mom was very strong, and she persevered through all the abuse she experienced growing up. She received good grades in school and graduated from high school without any support from her family. She continued on to college, but eventually withdrew due to the responsibility of taking care of her mom. Pearl managed the household because her mom's mental condition had gotten progressively worse.

Maudie was unable to pay bills or balance a checkbook. According to my mother, conversations with Maudie barely made any sense. It was very hard to follow her in a casual conversation.

There wasn't any intervention from outside the family. To Pearl's recollection, her mom didn't have any friends or close acquaintances. She was clearly a loner. In some ways, according to Pearl, her mom felt like a stranger even to her. She stated, "Mom never really felt like a mother to me."

CHAPTER 2

When Pearl Meets Jesse

Pearl accepted Jesus Christ at a very young age. She openly expressed her love for God. I use to hear my mother whisper, "Yes, Jesus," as if Christ were present in the room and speaking to her.

Pearl enjoyed going to church. In 1962, while singing in a choir, she met and later fell in love with Jesse McClure. They both attended a Baptist church on the South Side of Chicago. Pearl had a melodious voice, likened to an operatic songbird. Jesse sang with much passion, but his notes were usually off key.

There were many reasons Jesse was attracted to Pearl. She was very proper in her speech and mannerisms. Her smile was like the sun, and the love she exuded captivated anyone in her presence. She was intelligent, confident, sweet, pretty, and full of positive energy. Pearl wore conservative clothing with pizzazz! She was a full-figured woman who stood about five feet two. She had a beautiful, round face and big, gorgeous legs. Other guys were interested in Pearl, but she only had eyes for Jesse.

Jesse and Pearl often reminisced with smiles and laughter about singing in the choir together. It was cute listening to them tell funny stories about what happened in those days. The latter part of 1962, Pearl and Jesse got married and eventually had four children. There were three girls—Valerie, Billie Jean, and Patricia—and one boy, Jake. Although Pearl now had a family of her own, she was still responsible for caring for her mother. So Maudie lived with Pearl and her family until she passed away. Before Maudie's passing, everyone in the household was kept on high alert to look after Maudie. It was understood that she had a mental problem.

I have no recollection of my grandmother because she died when I was only two years of age. My mom told me stories about how she had to watch her mother around me because she was afraid Maudie would run off with me. Maudie felt we were her children, and she would try to dictate how Pearl should attend to us.

The McClure family endured many transitions as Maudie's caregivers. She was very combative and displayed peculiar behaviors. One time Maudie tried to put Pearl out of her own bedroom because she believed Jesse was her husband. Other times, Maudie left the house and didn't return for days. Back then, it was difficult to stop someone from coming and going, even if he or she had mental issues. The laws were different then, and there were limited resources. Pearl was always concerned about her mother when she went missing. Jesse scouted the neighborhood for Maudie. She was sometimes found sleeping on the streets or on the park bench as if she were homeless.

Regardless of Maudie's mental condition, Pearl always treated her with dignity and respect. Still, Pearl lived in fear, accepting the real possibility her mom could try to harm her family. She worried about finding Maudie dead or burning down the house, leaving her family with nowhere to go. These thoughts visited Pearl's mind on a regular basis, creating a growing anxiety.

My dad was very supportive in helping Mom take care of Maudie, and he echoed Pearl's claim of Maudie having a mental condition. Pearl often joked about how her mother found Jesse attractive. He was six feet one in stature, slender, and brown-skinned with hazel eyes. Most women who interacted with him described Jesse as very easy on the eyes and charismatic. He was always willing to give his opinion about any subject of conversation, even when it wasn't solicited. My father had a reputation of being a lady's man, but Pearl was in denial.

CHAPTER 3

Two Different Worlds

J esse and Pearl loved each other but had a tumultuous relationship because they were from two totally different worlds. Pearl grew up in a middle-class family, where she had family members who were well-cultured. Jesse migrated to Chicago from Little Rock, Arkansas, for better opportunities. He was a self-made man. Pearl used proper English while Jesse spoke in a drawling Southern vernacular and used broken English and profanity as part of his everyday repertoire. They had very little in common (an issue that became almost fatal in later years). My father was a true country boy and enjoyed living off the land, fishing and hunting for wild game. My mom was totally the opposite. She hated the outdoors and enjoyed dining in fabulous restaurants, going to plays and concerts, and traveling. I really had the best of both worlds. From the age of six, I spent a lot of time fishing with my dad and enjoying special events and fine dining with my mom.

Pearl delivered me at the age of thirty-seven, which was considered old at that time. Being the baby of the family, I had more responsibilities, but also many more opportunities. My mother exposed me to almost everything the city of Chicago had to offer, from ice skating to community/art festivals, from plays to concerts. If my family struggled financially, I was oblivious to it. I recall visiting and dining at the Palmer House, Lawrence Steakhouse, the Marriott Hotel, and the Water Tower Place with my mom. I use to thumb through the pages of the *Chicago Reader* to find the hottest events going on in the city for us to enjoy.

I relished shopping with my mom at the major department stores on State Street. We visited Montgomery Ward, Wieboldt's, and Sears on a regular basis. I vividly remember carrying shopping bags full of clothes. And why not? My father made decent money for that time. Not that he was going to use it. He worked at the steel mill, but he preferred shopping at the thrift stores. Pearl despised the fact that he bought everything there, and wanted her to purchase the kids' clothes there too. Pearl would buy Jesse underwear from the department store because she felt such personal items should be purchased new.

Clothing wasn't the only type of purchase Pearl and Jesse disagreed on. Pearl was cultured and ambitious. Her tenacity is what afforded my family the opportunity to purchase a nice home on the South Side. It was a spacious green-and-white three-bedroom house with a basement apartment. My dad fought with my mom every step of the way when she declared they would buy the house. But my mom tuned him out and did what she felt was best for the family. I lived in one residence all of my life until I moved out from under my parent's roof.

Everyone knew that Pearl was the glue that held the bonds together. She made sure all the bills got paid and that our family was comfortable. My dad made sure the family had food to eat, as he was too familiar with not having food and being hungry from his childhood. He planted a garden full of vegetables in the backyard and regularly visited another garden to purchase fresh fruits and more vegetables. We had two deep freezers, one full of meats and the other full of vegetables and beans. There was always food on the table, and our basic needs—coupled with some wants—were always met. My mother made it possible for us to have cable and a big color television set in the mid 1980s. I didn't know how fortunate I was until years later, when I realized that my mom was the one who'd made it all possible!

Everything on the outside of the McClure home looked very normal. However, looks can be deceiving. There were times when our home was the last place I wanted to be. My parents argued on a regular basis about his extramarital affairs and about their bills. In most cases, other arguments were preempted by arguments regarding the bills. I could never understand why my dad always went on a tirade about the bills when ultimately he knew the bills had to be paid. I recall wanting to confront my father about his idiotic behavior after many of the intense arguments. But I followed what I had been taught: "Honor thy father and thy mother: that thy days may be long upon the land which the Lord thy God giveth thee" (Ex. 20:12). There were times, however, when I considered running away. I made a vow that I would never marry a man who I would have to argue with about money. It was absolutely insane and caused unnecessary stress. After all, it was impossible to live and survive anywhere for free!

My father used to get upset because my mom made every Christmas huge and eventful for the children. Santa Claus was very generous to the McClure family, and my dad resented that. I have fond memories of Christmas Eve with my brother, Jake, listening to Nat King Cole while sipping on hot chocolate and baking cookies in brand-new pajamas and house shoes. My two older sisters were older and spent Christmas Eve with their friends. The Christmas tree overflowed with toys, clothes, electronics, board games, and more, and we had everything we could possibly imagine. I would go through catalogs at Christmas time and pick out whatever I wanted just to see if good old St. Nick would deliver. And he did every year.

Easter was a huge holiday for our family. My mom always bought us new clothes to wear to church. Before going to church, we would stand at the top of the porch on the step of our green-and-white house and take pictures. This became our family tradition, until there were so many pictures taken on Easter Sunday from the top stair of the porch that the years became confusing. My dad wasn't in any of the pictures. He was usually upset because he was against my mom buying us new outfits for Easter.

Pearl made a lot of sacrifices for her family. She would always say, "Parents have a responsibility to take care of their children because they didn't ask to be here." But as the years passed, it became ever more evident that my parents had very little in common and lived in two different worlds.

CHAPTER 4

World's Greatest Mom

P earl was always very loving and compassionate. These attributes were extended to those beyond her immediate family. I can recall my mother helping distant family members in financial crisis, visiting family members or friends in the nursing home, and giving someone in need clothes or food. My mom would even go out and purchase brand-new clothes for people who were in need. Her philosophy was, "You never give someone something that you wouldn't want."

My mother had a lot of compassion for women, especially single mothers. There were several times she offered rides to women she saw carrying groceries from the store. Sometimes they would have bags in one hand and young children in the other. I was scared because these people were really strangers, which went against the "stranger danger" rule I had been taught.

Unfortunately, my mother allowed herself to be taken advantage of quite often. There were relatives who called only when they wanted something. I can recall taking long bus rides on public transportation with my mother from the southwest side to the southeast side of Chicago to deliver groceries to alleged family members. I would gaze out the window or watch the different characters getting on and off the bus to help pass the time. I saw it all traveling on Chicago's buses and trains!

Unfortunately, once my mother and I arrived at our destination, many of the people didn't have enough decency to even say thank you for the groceries. For some reason, they had this feeling of entitlement—something that frustrated me a lot. But my mother believed that we should help others in need, especially family. Mom would always say that you don't do anything to hear "Thank you." You do it because it is the right thing to do and it's pleasing to God. She would remind me of Jesus' words: "For I was an hungred, and ye gave me meat: I was thirsty, and ye gave me drink: I was a stranger, and ye took me in" (Matt. 25:35).

My mother was extremely kind and had a heart of gold. But seeing how the family took advantage of my mother, I seized every opportunity to intercept such occurrences. When family called, I would answer the phone and be very sneaky with people who I knew wanted something. I either told them my mother wasn't home, or that I would give her the message, but I had no intentions to. The main caller was "Leeching Liz." She had a begging voice to go along with her phony script.

I can recall all the people who visited and how much I hated it. I looked forward to the day I'd move out of the family compound so I could be my true introverted self. After many years of witnessing my mom being taken advantage of, I decided very early on that I would not allow it to happen to me.

My mother spent a lot of time with her children. She was hands-on and functioned as a single parent. My father had a lot of resentment toward my mom because he felt she gave us too much attention. In retrospect, he was probably jealous. He used this as justification for his multiple extramarital affairs. My mom drowned out her unhappiness and depression in her marriage by spending a lot of time with us and taking vacations with her friends. She went on a vacation every year. I remember seeing her pictures from when she was in New York, California, Bahamas, Las Vegas, New Orleans and Mexico just to name a few.

Even with all the traveling, my parents' bad relationship started to affect my mother's mental health. I remember seeing my mother cry but didn't know why. There were other things too. One time I called out, "Mom?" to my mother like I always did. My mother had this weird look in her eyes and told me to stop calling her Mom. She said, "Call me Shirley," and she didn't give an explanation why. Shirley was actually her middle name. I thought the interaction was rather strange, but I continued to call her Mom anyway. Pearl's weird outburst never left my mind. When I finally brought this to my mother's attention, she had no recollection of the incident. Maybe she was just so tired and exhausted that day, she didn't realize what she'd said.

Pearl was a mother to the neighborhood. When she would take her children to the zoo, she allowed other children to go with her. She felt it was important for children to be exposed to different activities and events beyond their neighborhood. My mother took me for ice skating lessons at Lincoln Park Zoo. We traveled approximately two hours on public transportation just so I could learn how to skate. And the trips continued; I was one of the few kids from the community who learned how to ice skate. From that experience, I started going to Bicentennial Plaza in downtown Chicago to skate.

Pearl was very active and supportive with anything her children wanted to do. She was even a den mother for son Jake's Boy Scouts troop. Pearl took the Boy Scouts camping and on other field trips. She was also president of the PTA at her children's school and volunteered quite a bit. My mother was the president of the block club and a community activist. When local politicians ran for office, they would solicit Pearl's assistance with their campaigns. She was a leader and well respected by many. She had such an ability to influence others.

My father was very busy working and had little time for his family. In addition to his full-time job, he was a partner at an auto mechanic shop. Jesse was very skilled at working on cars, something he did on the side. Oddly enough, he was very private about his employment at his full-time job. We would sporadically visit him at the auto shop, but no one in the family ever laid eyes on the steel mill at which he worked. He never really talked about his full-time job. The mill would hold family outings, but he never invited our family to attend. His work phone number wasn't even listed as an emergency contact number for school, and no one knew how to contact him at work in the event of an emergency.

My father's job remained a mystery for the entire twenty years he was employed there. During my childhood, I didn't think much about this, but as I grew older, I realized something was wrong. He was hiding something!

Years later, when I was fourteen years old, the big secret was finally revealed. My dad fathered a child with a woman he worked with—the same time he had a child with my mom. My brother Jake was born one month a part from his love child. This explained why his job was a secret all of those years.

My father's infidelity continued to perpetuate my mom's stress and depression. Jesse fathering another child outside of the marriage hurt her deeply. She resented the fact that he didn't bond with Jake the way he should have. It might have been because he had two kids born the same year, but she didn't know that at the time. And Jesse's guilt got the best of him as time progressed. As a result, poor Jake paid the price and took the brunt of Jesse's misplaced anger.

Pearl started off working part-time as an office manager. She eventually went full time once we got older. She worked at one of the tallest skyscrapers in downtown Chicago. The office fostered a culturally diverse environment, and Pearl was well liked by her coworkers. The experience broadened her horizons and allowed her to introduce us to even more new opportunities. The more my mom experienced, the more she wanted for her children.

She also started to detach from Jesse emotionally. Pearl felt very lonely in her marriage, but she masked the hurt by staying busy. Jesse's infidelity affected her more than the world or her family could ever know. Sometimes Mom would sit and weep on the long brown couch in the living room. When I asked her what was wrong, she would say, "I'm okay, baby," with streams of tears rolling down her face.

My heart ached as I witnessed all the pain my father imposed upon my mother. I wanted to protect my mother from him. Thoughts of harming my dad visited my mind on a regular basis. It's only by the grace of God that I never acted on my thoughts.

I think the stress of me worrying about my mom led me to having seizures. My last seizure was when I moved out to go to college. Mom was the nicest person on earth, and for the life of me, I couldn't understand why my father treated her so badly. If only my mom would have listened. She was forbidden to marry my dad by his mother and sisters. It speaks volumes when a family member unequivocally advises you not to marry their loved one. If she had listened, it could have saved her from a life of heartache and pain at the hands of Jesse.

I loved my mom with every fiber of my being. She was my role model, except for when it came to relationships. I didn't like that my mom stayed with my dad even though he mistreated her. I remember wishing that they would get a divorce.

Mom persevered through her marital issues and continued to be a loving and supportive mother. She made it possible for me to attend John Robert Powers Acting School in downtown Chicago. This was big time in my mind! My acting instructor was an accomplished actress and beauty pageant winner. I am very grateful to my mom for this experience.

My mother made sure I had everything I needed to blend in with the culture of the actors and models. She dressed me in Izod shirts, khakis, penny loafers, and scarves. I came into contact with wealthy people when I ventured off in the Palmer House Hotel. I enjoyed listening to classical music being played on the grand piano in the huge, decorative, lavish lobby. My mom took me to the French Quarter Restaurant in the hotel to expose me to an exquisite ambiance.

From this experience, I was exposed to a different lifestyle. I developed an appetite for classical music. My mom had an eclectic appetite for music as well, which is how she drowned out her pain. I can appreciate almost every genre of music because of her. My interest in music is all over the spectrum. Mom and I would ride in the car, listening to Beethoven, Frank Sinatra, Dean Martin, Miles Davis, Temptations, Andy Gibb, Michael Jackson, New Edition and Barry Manilow. One of my mother's favorite songs from my generation was "Mama" by Boyz II Men. To this day, whenever I hear this song, I start to weep thinking about her.

I went on to grow my artistic talents and attended ETA Creative Arts Foundation, where I took theatre classes and the Katherine Dunham African Dance Technique. Eventually I performed in various theater productions. While a part of ETA Productions, I had the opportunity to visit Motown in Detroit, Michigan. My father was totally against me going to Motown for unknown reasons. In hindsight, I deduced that it was probably because he was having some control issues. He expressed that he had concerns with me traveling long distance in a van. Despite my father's apprehension, my mom stood up to him and allowed me to go. The trip was absolutely amazing and became an experience I will never forget! And I owe that all to my mom.

My mom was very supportive of my acting career, and she never missed a production despite working full-time and maintaining her household. I knew that I had the world's greatest mom, and she was truly my hero! I had decided that if I ever became a mom, I would follow her example. Currently, I find myself emulating my mom's attributes as a mother.

CHAPTER 5

Fighting with the Enemy

I n January 1991, I prepared to do what had never been
done before in the McClure family: go away to a school
that was two and a half hours from home. I made up
my mind to transfer colleges and go to a university downstate
in southern Illinois. I had always dreamed of going away to
escape from home. I knew that it was time for me to leave
the nest before I did something to my dad that I would later
regret.

I also knew I needed help preparing for financial aid.
My parents were unable to assist me in completing the
paperwork. So I went to a financial aid office to get help.
The office was located in the housing projects, and it came
highly recommended by other college students.

As I journeyed down the basement stairs, I felt as if I was
being led to a dungeon. It was very scary. The office light
was dim, and the door was a black gate that I could only
envision was like prison bars to a jail cell. The gentleman who
assisted me was a man who looked very intimidating. He was

ungroomed and missing one eye. I could hear my mother's voice in my head telling me not to stare.

The man was pessimistic during the process and acted as if he didn't want to be bothered. He laughed at me when I told him my major was psychology. When I got home, I told my mom how the man responded, and she said to blow it off. Mom told me, "Don't let it bother you." She reassured me that I was making the right decision to go away to college and told me that she was behind me 100 percent.

I was on my way out of the family compound and couldn't wait! Mom was happy for me too, yet at the same time disheartened about me leaving. I was the youngest out of the four of us, but my mom depended on me the most.

My dad was against me going away to college and majoring in psychology. He felt that psychology was "stupid" and didn't work. He had dreams of me becoming a lawyer, although he was not contributing a dime toward my education. I loved my mother dearly, but my feelings fluctuated for my dad. Like most children, I sided with my mom. My father's adulterous behavior had taken a toll on the family, and I was at my wit's end and ready to go.

As the years passed, Mom became more and more depressed. Her physically handicapped brother lived in our home, and caring for him kept her distracted and moving forward. Drew depended on his baby sister. In 1977, he had fallen down the stairs at the house while he was intoxicated. That fall left his mobility impaired and he lived with us for over 25 years.

The running joke in the family was that Drew was really Pearl's husband, because they did everything together.

They watched television, shared meals, laughed, and talked together. Some evenings on Mom's way home from downtown, she would pick up her brother's favorite dinner. He also smoked a pipe, and Pearl would buy him different types of tobacco from tobacco shops downtown. On any given day when you walked in our home, the room smelled of cinnamon spice, apple, cherry or strawberry pipe tobacco. You could hear the sound of my uncle sucking on his pipe, and see the smoke blowing into the air.

My dad resented the fact that Pearl and her brother were so close. Sometimes Drew would get into the middle of Pearl and Jesse's arguments and tell Jesse how he didn't like the way he treated his "baby sis," which is what he affectionately called Pearl. Drew would also tell women who called for Jesse not to call his sister's house. He didn't hold back in telling Jesse how disrespectful it was to have his women calling his baby sister's house.

At times, I would be so nervous, thinking that my father was going to hurt Drew. He was in a wheelchair and really wasn't in a position to defend himself. However, it was no secret that despite his handicap, Drew was incredibly strong. If Drew grabbed you, he was not letting you go. It's ironic that whenever anyone needed a jar opened, they always went to Drew.

When I visited from college, I noticed my mother's baseline appeared to be off. She was out of her character. My mom was normally strong, positive, and upbeat. But she was presenting as weak and hopeless. As much as I wanted to ignore it, I had to accept the fact that Pearl's depression had spiraled out of control. In addition, Mom was starting to have problems with her memory. She would repeat herself over and over again. When anyone brought it to her attention, she became very defensive. But it was true. Notes were posted all around the house—on the refrigerator, on her bedroom mirror, in the dining room, and in the kitchen. After all, Mom had a lot on her plate, and it was hard for her to remember everything. She took care of her brother, whose needs were very demanding. And she was still there for all of my older siblings. Even with a troubled marriage, it was truly amazing to see how Mom held it all together for so long.

My parents made it to my college campus on a few occasions. Initially, my mother helped to move me in the dorm. Pearl was such a proud mother. On a separate occasion, she came down for my sorority pinning ceremony along with my sister, Billie Jean. Mom visited once again, this time accompanied by my father for Parents' Weekend. The Temptations were performing that weekend. My dad was happy because we had great seats. He was also proud because I was a member of the university student board.

My parents stayed with me at my apartment, and I was so happy to host them for the weekend. My dad didn't complain, and my mom was holding her own. Her memory was on point the entire weekend. It was a wonderful time, one that I will never forget.

In December of 1993, I called my mother to share with her how excited I was about my graduation ceremony. I anticipated my mom and dad coming down for the occasion. Instead Mom asked me, "Would you be upset if I didn't attend your graduation?" Mom explained that she didn't want to listen to my dad complain in the car about "any and everything." She further added that she didn't want to leave her brother Drew.

Although I knew one of my siblings could look after Uncle Drew, I told her that I understood. I masked the hurt by pretending I was fine. But deep down inside, I was crushed. I ended the call, careful not to give into my emotions while still on the phone. When I hung up, I began to cry hysterically until I made myself sick. I eventually cried myself to sleep.

I knew from my mother's reluctance to attend the ceremony that her mental condition had deteriorated. If she had all of her mental faculties, there was no way she would suggest missing my college graduation ceremony.

I eventually informed my dad that Mom had said she wouldn't be attending the graduation. He assured me that Mom would be there. It turned out that my mom did attend the graduation, but she was very quiet. I knew my mother was happy for me on the inside. I wondered if my mom had to endure my dad's verbal abuse—ranting and raving with all his foolishness—during that two and a half hour car ride, and I felt sorry for her.

As I started educating myself about the stages of Alzheimer's, it appeared my mom was in the early stages, possibly Stage 3—Mild Cognitive Decline. Mom no longer remembered people with whom she had previously interacted. It was obvious that during conversations, Pearl was lost. She tried to cover it up by smiling and nodding her head.

I was embarrassed, but sucked it up. After all, this was my mother. My dad had always told me, "You should never be embarrassed of your parents."

CHAPTER 6

The Prelude to the Unwanted Guest!

After graduation, I moved back home to start my career. The notes and memos posted around the house had grown more intense. The amount of notes had tripled. My mother's memory was getting worse. She appeared more and more disorganized, moody, and withdrawn. She needed assistance with managing her finances but was in denial. My mother was now entering into what I thought was Stage 4 of Alzheimer's. She was experiencing a moderate cognitive decline. During this stage, my mother's bad days started to outweigh her good days. And this started to take a toll on me.

Sometimes when Mom and I were out, she would run into old acquaintances. Mom would suggest to them that they get together for lunch or dinner. This disturbed me so much because I felt Mom was giving people false hope. Looking back, I don't know why I allowed it to bother me. After all, the people she was extending the invitation to probably didn't even give it much thought. They were probably agreeing just to be nice. I should have just chalked it up to meaningless conversation. During this stage, my mother's behaviors became more and more bizarre.

Mom and my sister, Billie Jean, rode the CTA bus wearing big, silly character hats (i.e. Dr. Seuss) and carrying teddy bears in their arms. They were amused that people found them weird. I was furious about the whole idea and hoped no one I knew would run into them. Pearl and Billie Jean indicated how much they enjoyed watching people's reaction. Although Billie Jean wasn't officially diagnosed with a mental illness, I knew that my sister's behavior wasn't normal. She was extremely bright and intelligent, but was inflicted with societal issues that altered her behavior. Billie Jean's decision-making skills and judgment caused me to question her cognitive skills. She danced to the music and drums that only played in her head.

Mom started having problems with her knees and couldn't do all of the walking that she use to do. The doctor recommended surgery initially on her left knee. The doctor wanted to hold off doing surgery on both knees at one time. After surgery, Mom was off work for an extended period of time, recovering. Pearl had been at her job as an office manager for over fifteen years. She had a lot of tedious tasks to remember and perform. One day, Pearl's friend and coworker called and asked if the family had noticed anything different about her. She continued to describe how Pearl was forgetting to complete tasks at work, and it was becoming very noticeable to others at the workplace. Consequently, my mom started to complain about how she didn't like her boss; she felt that her boss was out to get her. That was totally out of character for my mom. She didn't talk about people and wasn't the paranoid type. Mom had always spoken very highly about her supervisor. As time went on, she became more and more forgetful. She started to have difficulty remembering what she had done from week to week and then from day to day. When this was brought to her attention, she would get mad and become very defensive.

My parent's arguments grew more intense because Mom was losing her cognitive skills and abilities. It became even more difficult for her to explain her reasoning for certain financial decisions she made. She wasn't capable of defending herself to my dad. This really concerned me, especially because I knew what my dad was capable of if he got upset. As secrets about past financial transactions started to unravel, my father got extremely angry. He started to feel as if he was deceived! The truth of the matter is, my mom kept a lot of information from him during their marriage because of his lack of knowledge in running a household. He was extremely difficult to deal with and unreasonable. My mom would always say, "This house would cave in if it wasn't for me."

As time went on, my mom problem with her right knee became worse and the doctor had no other choice but to operate. After this surgery, she went on short-term disability from work, which eventually turned into long-term disability. Mom never returned to her job after the second knee surgery. I was so grateful that her employer allowed her to bow out gracefully. However, the more time Pearl spent at home, the more it seemed the Alzheimer's progressed. A lot of this had to do with the fact that she was out of her daily routine. I learned that patients with Alzheimer's need a routine and change is not good for them. Surely, the arguing and interrogation by my dad definitely didn't help her mental state either. My father and siblings were all in denial. Sometimes people would prefer to remain in denial because that means they don't have to do anything. I believe I was the only family member who acknowledged that something was wrong with Pearl. My awareness and acceptance came from working in the behavioral health care field and being around residents with Alzheimer's.

I recognized that my mother's illness was progressing. So I started taking her out of town to visit relatives that she had close relationships with over the years. My dad was very upset because he didn't want her to go for his own selfish reasons. He also knew that relatives resented the way he treated her. We went to California to visit my dad's family, who adored my mom. Later we went to North Carolina for my aunt's retirement party and had a wonderful time. Pearl rose to the occasion by pretending she knew everyone in attendance. My mom and aunt married two brothers. Mom worked the room like the true social butterfly she was, and no one really knew that her cognitive functioning was affected.

While living at home, I started to assume the responsibility for more of my mother's personal affairs because she verbalized, "I do not trust Jesse." So I began to help mom make sound decisions. Pearl started to openly express her disdain for my father. She made it very clear to me that if she were to ever reach a point where she was very sick and unable to make decisions for herself, she didn't want my dad to make any decisions on her behalf. She went to great lengths to legally ensure that my father wouldn't be able to make any decisions about her life, including appointing me as power of attorney of health care. She expressed to me that she wouldn't be surprised if Jesse tried to kill her. I was hurt that my mom would say something like that about my dad, but she knew him very well! That thought often lingered in my mind because my dad had a gun collection because he was a hunter.

Mom eventually admitted to me that she knew she was having problems with her memory and how much it bothered her. But she downplayed it all at the same time by stating she wasn't perfect. Mom stated that she felt my dad was having problems with his memory as well. She verbalized her final wishes to me on a regular basis, saying that if she ever got really sick and her quality of life was affected, to just let her go. Mom was very explicit in the fact that she did not want any machines keeping her alive. It was as if she were predicting her own death. I was so grateful that my mother spoke so openly about her final wishes, but I couldn't imagine ever having to carry them out.

In 1995, I decided that it was time for me to move into my own apartment. I was very tired of all the drama at the family compound. I wanted my own space and serenity, but I would still be there for Mom. My parents were sad when I announced that I was moving out to the suburbs. This was a very difficult decision for me because I felt I was abandoning my mother. But at the same time, I was ready to go. I'd had enough! Part of me felt like I was being punished for my mother's bad decision to marry my dad. I also resented the fact that my mother stayed with him despite her own unhappiness. I believe the bad marriage contributed to my mom's mental decline.

My siblings didn't appear to be affected by Mom's mental condition because they were all consumed with their own personal problems. My mother expressed to me that she felt abandoned by everyone and was very lonely living in the house. She was so used to her children being around. I was the baby of the family and the last one to leave the nest. So this was a huge transition for Mom. Although my mom wasn't very happy, it was a good decision for me. I enjoyed the solace I had in my own apartment. I didn't realize the amount of stress that I was under until I moved out on my own.

While sitting in the bathroom in my own apartment one day, I realized how quiet it was. No one was knocking or yelling through the door to "get out." I recall sitting there for about thirty minutes with tears of joy because I couldn't believe that I wasn't interrupted. I started thanking God for peace. At that very moment, I knew that I could never move back home because the peace was priceless. I was a true introvert; I enjoyed peace and quiet and very little company. For so many years, I was forced to deal with company and noise because I had no other alternative. I finally had an opening to experience serenity. Living alone, I was also able to pray and praise God in a way that I never had before. "Thou will keep him in perfect peace, whose mind is stayed on thee: because he trusteth in thee" (Isaiah 26:3).

I spoke with my parent's separately on a daily basis. When I spoke to my dad, he reminded me that my mother's mind wasn't good. I knew there was some truth to what he was saying, but I took it with a grain of salt. I felt my dad had mental health issues too. He was a product of growing up too fast and having too many responsibilities at such a young age. My dad was a very complex man with a lot of baggage from his childhood. At times, he was in denial about my mom having Alzheimer's, but at other times, he acknowledged something was wrong with her. Sometimes he would say, "She's pretending because she doesn't want to be held accountable for the decisions she made in the past." To a logical person, most of the things my dad said did not make any sense. Dad was extremely difficult to reason with, and he enjoyed having an audience when he spoke.

My father was very nosey and always had an opinion about someone else's situation. There was a double standard in how he lived and how he expected others to live. Dad had some major issues with God, which also complicated his marriage. Mom was saved and had a strong relationship with God. She accepted Jesus as her Lord and savior, attended church, prayed on a regular basis, and lived as righteously as she possibly could. My dad's faith was tested when a relative he prayed for passed away. It left him very bitter, and as a result, he stopped attending church.

Jesse felt that he was the king of his castle and the ruler of his domain. I had a major problem with this because I felt he was so undeserving, but at the same time, I adored him. My emotions regarding my father were always conflicted. I was mad at him most of the time for not treating my mother right. However, he was good to me as a father. For my dad's sixtieth birthday I went all out to show him how much I appreciated him. I coordinated a birthday celebration for him all by myself. He was dressed in a stylish gray and black suit with silver cufflinks that I purchased from Oak Tree. He wore a black-brimmed hat and a long black dress coat. My dad gazed at his wrist a few times that evening to look at his scintillating watch trimmed in diamonds. He had a clean shave and a fresh haircut, and he smelled of gray flannel cologne. He danced the night away with my mom, family and friends. My father said, "This is the best and only birthday party I have ever had." That was a night I would never forget because that night it appeared I had the perfect parents.

CHAPTER 7

The Unwanted Guest Arrives!

M y dad had moments when he was very protective and thoughtful as a father, but he wasn't attentive and loving as a husband. I learned how to separate the relationships in my mind to keep from hating him. Due to my mom's depression, her doctor requested that she see a psychologist. At her appointment, the psychologist asked her several questions. Her responses raised a red flag. The psychologist asked, "What year were you born?" "Who is the governor of Illinois?" and "Who is the president of the United States?"

Mom responded in a very snippy tone, "I don't know the day or the date I was born because it's not important." She believed President John F. Kennedy was the current president, but it was Bill Clinton, and she could not care less who the governor was. Then she replied that Mayor Jane Byrne was the governor of Illinois. I proceeded to correct my mom, but the psychologist stopped me. I was in a state of shock from my mom's responses. But at the same time,

I knew all along that something was wrong. My mother became uncooperative when the psychologist asked other questions. Mom basically flipped the psychologist off and the session ended rather abruptly.

In 1997, my mom was formally diagnosed with Alzheimer's, although she had been showing signs for a while. I felt my mother was now in Stage 5, which is Moderately Severe Decline. Alzheimer's is such an ugly disease. It was the guest that I hoped would never formally arrive. There was a part of me that wanted to believe that it was just depression affecting my mom's memory. I believed if the doctors were able to get that under control, my mom would be okay. Unfortunately, I had to deal with what I had been dreading for years. Alzheimer's is genetic. My grandmother Maudie had senility which diminished her cognitive level of functioning. I also thought that my dad was showing signs of dementia, but his symptoms weren't as profound as my mom's. I pray on a regular basis to break the curse of Alzheimer's and dementia. I also try to eat healthy, exercise, get my rest, and take vitamins to prevent it. The thought of getting Alzheimer's is very scary to me.

Mom continued to have follow-up appointments with her doctor from her last knee surgery, and she had to go see the psychologist on a bi-weekly basis. In all of her sessions with the psychologist, she would complain about my dad and how much she disliked him. Mom revealed in a session that my dad was never at home and that there was never any food in the house. This became an immediate concern for the psychologist, and she wanted me to investigate. Her concern was urging me to call the Department of Aging. My mother routinely vocalized her anger towards Jesse at almost every session and described him as an "evil man" and a "cheater." She made it very clear on numerous occasions that she was unhappy in her marriage.

I invited my oldest sister, Valerie, to a session, so she could hear all the bad things that Mom was saying about Dad. I was actually shocked that my mother was being so candid and wanted someone else in the family to hear how she felt. My mother shared with the psychologist that Jesse had been questioning her about old bills and receipts that he'd found. She further stated that he would talk crazy when she couldn't recall any specifics about the documentation. Mom stated that Dad was bringing women into the house, talking dirty to women over the phone in her company, leaving her for long hours by herself with no food, and was very rough with her in the bedroom. Mom suspected that he was probably watching pornography. Mom said, "I hate having sex with him." I was in a difficult situation. How do you begin to tell your dad that your mom is not happy with him in the bedroom? It was obvious that my mom had changed because I couldn't believe she even shared that with me. She was always so private. My mother advised me not to confront my dad, but it really bothered me. I was uncertain how to handle this because I didn't want to risk losing a relationship with my dad, who I also loved. Sometimes parents can put you in peculiar situations.

When I attended the sessions and answered the psychologist's questions truthfully, my mother would get upset. My sister Valerie wasn't as truthful about her observations, because she didn't want Mom to be mad at her.

They had a very close relationship and were more like sisters than mother and daughter. I had more of a parental role with my mother. I always left the session feeling like the bad guy. To avoid telling the psychologist the truth in front of my mom, I would write the psychologist a note with an update. I wrote the note prior to the session and honestly reported my mom's status. I really wanted Valerie to take over since they were closer. I got tired of feeling like the bad person. In some ways, I felt my mom started to dislike me because I was always the bearer of bad news.

In 1997, an opportunity became available for me to move to southern Illinois. It was a promotion and a great strategic move for my career. But I was confused about accepting the offer because of my mom's condition. However, I knew if I didn't take the promotion, I could be stifling my career. Plus it was time for me to let another family member step up to the plate. I became regional director for a behavioral healthcare organization and moved into corporate housing in downstate Southern Illinois. After I relocated, I stayed in close contact with my oldest sister to ensure that Mom got everything she needed. Valerie was responsible for confirming that mom had the foods she wanted to eat. Valerie wasn't employed, so she took Mom to the mall every day. It was her responsibility to take Mom to all of her doctor appointments. For important doctor visits, I would come up from down state to accompany her. My dad was upset because he felt Mom and Valerie were spending too much money. I felt that my mother had a right to spend her money freely because she had worked all those years and deserved it.

In the early months of 1999, Mom's condition got progressively worse. She started having problems with her active daily living skills. She also had problems controlling her bladder, eating, and sleeping. She had started wandering through the neighborhood. Consequently, Uncle Drew's health began failing too, and he later died in May of 1999. After Drew's death, Mom went into a deeper depression and her mental state continued to decline. It appeared that the medications mom was taking were no longer effective. My mother's condition eventually became too much for Valerie to manage. They were very close, but Valerie didn't know how to redirect our mother, because mom had always rescued her. Their relationship was dysfunctional in a lot of ways. Reality had started to set in. I knew that I would have to move back home to take care of my mother before a tragedy happened. My reality was confirmed through prayer. Everything lined up so smoothly for me to return home. My old job called and asked me to come back, instituting a higher salary. I was able to live in corporate housing in a high-rise apartment building in Hyde Park until I reestablished a permanent residence in the Chicago land area. I enjoyed waking up in the apartment and looking at the Chicago skyline in the early morning. Though I loved it, I later moved in with one of my sorority sisters, and shortly thereafter, discretely married an old childhood sweetheart.

CHAPTER 8

Naughty by Nature

Mom called me several times per day indicating that she was hungry and that there was no food in the house. When I confronted Jesse, he told me that there was food in the house but Pearl was "too picky." I attempted to explain to my dad that they have always had differences in their choice of foods, and he couldn't expect her to eat various types of wild game, beans, and pork. He knew my mom had never been a fan of deer meat, squirrel, raccoon, or rabbit. There was no getting through to this man! It was "his way or the highway" as he would often proclaim. So I started buying my mom groceries that required no cooking and minimum preparation because she was no longer able to cook. She had previously left the stove burners on and pots unattended, which could have caused a fire. My father would remove the knobs on the stove when he would leave home to prevent Mom from turning on the stove.

My mother shared with me on several occasions that she was at home by herself. With her diagnosis of depression too, it was not a good idea for her to be left at home for long periods of time. Mom had my phone number ingrained in her mind. She had a hard time remembering other phone numbers, which is why she called me so frequently throughout the day. Sometimes she would forget that she had called me and would call again and have the same exact conversation. When she called, Mom complained about my dad taking fishing trips with his girlfriends and running the streets. Neighbors even started to call me to report they observed my mom standing in the hallway for long periods of time by herself. Her unannounced strolls through the neighborhood became more frequent and longer. I was very nervous thinking one day my mom wouldn't find her way back home, or worse, she'd be killed.

Mom told me that my dad had a neighbor in the basement apartment of their home. She was certain that an indiscretion had occurred between my dad and the neighbor. My mom had known this lady for years. They used to borrow food items from each other, such as, butter, sugar, flour, etc. Our families interacted on a regular basis throughout the years. Mom had always suspected something between the two of them, so she wasn't shocked! When I confronted my dad about these accusations, he denied it. He admitted that Odessa was in the house, but nothing inappropriate had happened. Dad contended that he and Odessa were only having a drink, and that was it! Although mom was struggling with Alzheimer's, I believed my mom. I even recalled seeing Odessa and my father in the backyard, talking over the fence, when I was younger, and questioned their relationship. I started to feel more uneasy about my mother's living situation, but didn't know quite how to handle it. I was seriously contemplating calling the elder abuse and neglect hotline on my dad. My mom had started to lose weight, and it was like pulling teeth to get her to change her clothes or wear clothes appropriate for the season. These occurrences were attributed to her having Alzheimer's.

One day Mom called me and told me that my dad had physically jumped on her. She said he ran across credit card bills that she wasn't able to explain and just went crazy! Mom had several credit cards and made withdrawals from her 401K account, unbeknownst to my dad. She used a lot of her resources years ago to have repairs made to the house. My father never got anything repaired or painted. He was very cheap! All he did was complain about what needed to be done, but he wasn't going to do anything to fix the problem. If he did, it would not have been fixed the right way.

I called my father and confronted him again about his behavior. My parents had physical altercations in the past; but the difference now was that she couldn't defend herself. I told my dad that neighbors had called me and expressed concerns about Mom's safety. I warned him that it was only a matter of time before they called the elderly hotline on him for abuse. I was very concerned and knew that I was going to have to do something. I wonder if the time had finally come for me to call the elderly abuse hotline. The struggle was with my siblings pretending as if everything was fine. I was very frustrated and hated that I was even born into this family. I knew calling the hotline would destroy my relationship with my father and possibly the entire family. It appears that I got through to my dad because he never put his hands on her again. However, he continued to be verbally confrontational.

One day in late June of 1999, Valerie called me and told me that when she picked up our mother, she could barely walk. I was furious! *What has he done to her?* I thought. So I called my mother to find out what happened. She told me, "Jesse hurt me badly in the bedroom," and then asked me if I would come and pick her up. Mom said that he was doing all kinds of naughty stuff to her in the bedroom and she was scared. When I picked her up, it was obvious that she was having a hard time walking. Whatever he did to her in the bedroom impeded her walking ability. She had an undesirable body odor and her clothes were dirty. I couldn't wait to give my father a piece of her mind! Here was a woman who took pride in her hygiene and physical appearance, reduced to a person who looked homeless. My mom smelled awful! I also noticed that she had lost even more weight. When I picked her up, she immediately announced that she wasn't going back. Mom said that she was afraid that Jesse would kill her. She told me, "I would rather live in a nursing home than live with this evil man." I had been praying and asking God for guidance. I didn't know what to do, but I knew my mother couldn't go back. I was thinking about how I would tell my new husband that my mother was coming to live with us. I was confused about how to even approach the situation but I knew I had to protect my mom. When I told my husband, Blake, what was going on, he suggested that she live with us. Thank you God! From his own observation of her condition and the things that she was saying, Blake was very concerned. He told me to do whatever I thought was best, and he was with me all the way.

I thought after a few days my mom was going to change her mind, but as time went on, it appeared that she got more confident in her decision. Every day she consistently stated that she wasn't going back to Jesse. Blake strongly suggested that Pearl call Jesse and tell him herself that she wasn't coming back home. He advised me to stay out of their marriage because my parents were the ones who made their vows before God. Blake is a minister and it was important for him to ensure that everything was done decently and in order. Mom eventually called my dad and informed him that she wasn't going to return home. She said to him, "You are evil, there was never any food in the house, and you were never at home." She talked about all his extramarital affairs and the fact that he started bringing women into their home as if she was stupid. He took a lot of fishing trips with women. My dad was trying to control my mom. She talked about his rage and the "red" in his eyes, which I never quite understood. She was married to him, so maybe she could see something that I couldn't. From Pearl's responses on the call with my dad, it was obvious that he was making her a lot of promises on the other end of the phone, but Pearl wasn't budging. Jesse was very angry because that meant he would no longer have access to Pearl's finances. He was infuriated by this because there were so many things he wanted to do with her money. It appeared that he felt she owed him in some strange and warped way.

My father expressed how upset he was with my mom and me to other family members. He said, "I'm supposed to be taking a red bow off of my brand-new Lincoln at this stage in my life. Pearl messed all of that up!" It became more and more evident that my father really missed my mom's money. Sometimes I questioned if he really missed being around her. Did he really love her? One thing was for sure: he was upset because he had no one else to control. I was very happy but very overwhelmed about the responsibility of taking care of my mother. I hadn't been married that long, and taking care of my mom, being a newlywed, and planning a wedding ceremony all at the same time was very difficult. However, I was happy because I didn't have to worry about my mom being mistreated anymore.

Jesse attempted to call the house a few times. He would leave threatening messages on the voice mail—that is until my husband Blake called him and put a stop to it. Jesse thought I was stopping my mom from calling him, but after over thirty years, she had enough. Blake made it very clear to my dad that he was more than welcome to call our home, but that he couldn't call and threaten me. It was hard for Jesse to oblige, so he stopped calling. That was the beginning of a bitter and estranged relationship between my father and me.

CHAPTER 9

Lifestyle Shift

Blake and I were working out the details for our wedding ceremony. Jesse refused to give me away because I allowed my mother to come and live with me. My half-brother, who is also the oldest out of all my father's children, was suppose to give me away but was a no-show at the wedding. I figured he didn't show up because he didn't want to be on the outs with our father. I later heard through other family members that he couldn't make it because he had a migraine headache.

Things had gotten so bad with the break up between my parents that I attempted to get an order of protection put in place against my dad. I back-peddled hoping that he would come to his senses, so the order was never executed. My dad was acting out emotionally. He even sent me a threatening letter in the mail alluding to killing me on my wedding day. Fortunately, the letter didn't arrive until the Monday after the wedding. I thank God that the letter was delayed. I would not have been able to enjoy my wedding day if I had received the letter prior to my ceremony. I believe the impetus behind my dad's actions was that he felt I took my mom away from him. He could never get it through his thick and stubborn skull that it was her decision. She even told him, but he couldn't accept it. For so long, Mom had tolerated his crazy behavior and indiscretions. He found it hard to believe that it had all come to an end! The king had no one else to rule.

Mom's youngest brother, John, also contacted my dad to tell him that Pearl had expressed to him that she no longer wanted to be with him. John said that Jesse was very upset and he started using profanity over the phone. Extended family members told me that my dad felt I betrayed him. It really bothered me that I had to give up my relationship with my dad, with whom I was also very close at one point in time. I often reflect on the evening I picked mom up, I had no idea it would turn into a permanent situation. I knew something had to change but didn't know how and when. My mom was very clear about what she wanted to do. She expressed to me that she did not want to live with Jesse anymore. The night she came to live with us was a total surprise. I had to buy my mom clothes, underwear, shoes, toiletries and a bedroom set. Ironically, we had enough room for my mom to live with us. We lived in a nice two bedroom/two bath apartment in the suburbs. The interesting part is we later discovered that an adult day care was less than two miles from our home.

My husband and I were both employed full-time, so in the beginning we paid Valerie to sit with mom. This arrangement was only temporary. One of my colleagues advised me about my options and recommended I contact Department of Aging. I called and requested a DONS Assessment (Determination of Needs Functional Assessment). The assessment helped to determine the type of services my mom would need. Mom was assessed and she met the criteria for adult day care services. We visited several facilities before carefully making a selection. Blake and I were most happy with the facility located less than two miles away from our home. We felt they offered the best services. The facility used to be a residential home and was retrofitted, so it really felt like home. Initially, my mom was upset about going to a day care for adults. However, as time went on, she got used to it and started to enjoy it. My mom found comfort in being able to help others at the facility. She loved it! Mom also had an opportunity to do arts and crafts, play bingo, and participate in other recreational activities. I dropped my mom off before I went to work each day, and Blake picked her up in the evening after work. It was just like having the responsibility of a child.

Mom was always very fond of Blake, and he could do no wrong in her eyes. Blake and I met in high school, and my mom was impressed by his chivalrous ways. He showered my mom with love and affection. Blake and my mom were allies whenever they had a disagreement with me. Sometimes I felt like they would gang up on me. When Blake picked Mom up in the evening, he would drop the top on his black Camaro. They would ride off into the wind, listening to old music and singing to the top of their lungs. When they arrived home, Blake would prompt her to take her bath, and after that, he served her dinner. Sometimes Mom refused to eat what was served and demanded something different. Rather than trying to explain to her that it was important for her to eat healthy, he would defer her to me. Blake and I had several arguments about my mom and what she wanted for dinner. She wanted to eat fried fish and turkey burgers every day. My mother loved McDonald's and Burger King's fish sandwiches. It was very difficult getting her to understand that she couldn't eat fried fish every day because of her high cholesterol. She was also afflicted with diabetes and high blood pressure. I think sometimes Blake would give her whatever she wanted if I wasn't around. It was hard for him to be firm with her. Deep down inside, I think Blake really felt sorry for her. He loved her like a mother and didn't know how to stand his ground against her.

There were some unpleasant tasks associated with caring for my mother. I had to get use to pricking her finger to check her glucose. I had to take her to see a dietician on a regular basis to help her understand why she was on a special diet. I also wanted to take some of the pressure off of myself. I got tired of being the only one telling her what she couldn't eat. What the dietician told my mother went in one ear and out the other. So eventually I stopped taking her because she wasn't absorbing the information that the dietician was giving her. Having to be the person to enforce the rules all the time was hard. I had to stay focused on doing whatever was in my mother's best interest, and that wasn't always easy!

The role of caregiver had its challenges. On one occasion, I had to assist my mother in collecting a bowel specimen per doctor's order. The specimen was to be sent to the lab for testing. I wanted to believe so badly that she could do it on her own. After I came to the realization that she couldn't, I had to go in the bathroom with Pearl when she moved her bowels. I held the container to catch her feces as she used the bathroom. It was one of the grossest things that I ever had to do, but that was my mom. I had to transfer the feces into another container and then drop it off at the doctor's office. All of her results came back normal. Thank God, because the process wasn't easy!

Blake and I had very limited support in taking care of Mom. She rarely spent any time with Valerie anymore due to Valerie having her own personal problems. Valerie was no longer able to handle Mom's condition. I realized years later that Valerie had a very difficult time dealing with Mom's illness but didn't know how to express it. Blake was a huge help with my mother. Prior to me getting married, I was already scheduled to go on a cruise with one of my best friends, and Blake took care of my mom for the whole week. I was so fortunate to have such a supportive husband.

Blake and Mom had a very special bond, and they really enjoyed each other's company. Sometimes my mother would tell me that she thought I was too hard on Blake. Mom and Blake watched television together, and when he drifted off to sleep, she sat on the couch watching over him. I personally thought that this was a little creepy, but it didn't seem to bother Blake. When I arrived home in the evening from work, Mom would gesture to me to be quiet because Blake was resting. My mother felt it was her job to protect Blake while he was sleeping.

My mother and I spent a lot of time talking. Pearl was my mother but also my best friend. Even with Alzheimer's, she was still encouraging and a good listener. I enjoyed having my mother around most of the time, but some days it wasn't so nice. On her good days, Mom spoke with such wisdom. One day she offended me and told me that I was a killjoy. She pointed out to me that Blake was a dreamer and that I should let him dream instead of getting mad at him every time he said something that I thought was outlandish. After reflecting on what Mom had said, I realized she was right. From that moment on, every time Blake said something to me that I thought wasn't realistic, I remained silent and smiled.

One day Mom told me the biggest mistake that she ever made with me was not teaching me the value of the word *no*. I was stunned! For someone with Alzheimer's, she could really be insightful at times. There is value in the word *no* because you won't hear *yes* all the time, my mom exclaimed. She watched me struggle early in my marriage with having to compromise and share, two things she never taught me how to do. Although, I grew up with three other siblings in the house, I never had to share unless it was by choice. I grew up having my own clothes, snacks, personal belongings, money, etc. In some ways, my mom must have felt partially responsible, so she tried to encourage me during one of the most challenging times in my life.

Although my mom's good days outweighed the bad, it was important for her to stay connected with family and friends. But sometimes this came with many challenges and more problems. One Sunday after church, I was taking my mom over to her brother's house for dinner. John was a master chef by profession, and he was very anal. He was an excellent cook by all accounts and was well known for his craft. I called him to let him know that we would be late but would be there soon. I explained to him that Pearl was having a really bad day. She had an accident at church, and I had to clean her up before we came over. Uncle John was very upset about us running late. He stated that the food was already at 165 degrees and our unanticipated late arrival was messing things up. Blake was furious! He didn't want us to go after the way Uncle John had responded. If anyone should have been sensitive to what we were going through, it should have been her brother. But John was known for being extremely selfish and cut from a different cloth. He was the brother everyone avoided.

During my first rodeo in graduate school, Uncle John had a serious car accident that resulted in him having neck surgery. He had a medical device surrounding his head to hold it in place. It resembled a halo. John had a fiancé, and they had no children together. I spent a lot of time going back and forth to the hospital and to the doctor's office, tending to him. I only did it because of my mom. As a result, I had to drop out of graduate school because I missed too many days.

Throughout the years, all I ever heard from Uncle John and his fiancé was how nobody was there when he had his accident. This really infuriated me because I sacrificed my education to help him. I also asked my husband to go over to Uncle John's house several times to help him out with things around the house. But John and his fiancé never expressed any gratitude. So after that, I decided that I wasn't going to take on any more of my mother's monkeys. However, to keep the peace and to appease my mother, I took her to her brother's house for dinner that Sunday. During the course of the meal, John dropped subtle hints about how much he paid for the food. I couldn't believe it! So I gave my uncle a donation toward the food, knowing that it would be the last visit to his home for dinner. John served the family as if we were in a restaurant. He gave us a portion size of each food item and everyone knew not to ask for seconds, even if we were still hungry. John treated his kitchen as if the Department of Public Health were present. We did not touch the refrigerator to even get water. The food was delectable but no one felt free to move around like you would at a family member's home. John had some very funny ways, and he wasn't the easiest person to get along with.

Sometimes Pearl's oldest brother, Patrick, and his companion would invite her to extravagant dinners at banquet halls. I always bought Mom an outfit to wear so she could attend. Although the tickets were very costly, I felt my mom deserved it. I was willing to let my mother participate in anything that would allow her to be connected to her peers and have a great time. It didn't matter what it cost! That's what my mom worked so hard for all of those years! I wanted her to enjoy her retirement. Sometimes Mom would stay the night over at her brother's house, but as the Alzheimer's progressed, this became more difficult. I started to recognize her set- backs when her routine was disrupted. A change in an Alzheimer's patient's schedule isn't good because it only exacerbates their mental condition. It is strongly encouraged by professionals to have Alzheimer's patients on a routine schedule.

CHAPTER 10

It Is What It Is!

I never would have thought in a million years that I would be taking care of my mother. It was extremely difficult because I literally became a caregiver overnight for the woman I admired my whole entire life. How could this be happening to the woman who made it all happen for everyone else? How could this be happening to my hero? Sometimes I would start crying when I thought about how the tables had turned. Mom spent her whole life taking care of others, and now she had to be taken care of. The sad part is that she didn't really have people there for her the way she had always been there for them. This really troubled me, and it only confirmed that my mom was a true saint!

Time was approaching quickly for our wedding ceremony. Very few people knew that we were already married and living together. It was great for me to have my mother around during one of the most important events of my life. Although Mom had Alzheimer's, she was fully aware of what was going on and offered her opinion even when I didn't want it. My mother was right most of the time. She stressed to me not to overdo it because she said you have to have finances after the wedding is over. I kept this in perspective as I made plans for my wedding. I remember working really hard to shed some pounds before my big wedding day, and my mom was very encouraging. She was also involved in the wedding planning. Mom went shopping with me for all of my wedding items and attended all of my dress fittings.

Mom started crying at one of my dress fittings. It touched her to see me in my wedding gown. I was so grateful because it appeared that God allowed her to be a mom when I needed her the most. The relationship got confusing at times because of my various roles as a daughter, caregiver, and friend. But I was so glad to have her as mom at that time. I was also proud because I resembled my mom the most out of all my siblings.

I wanted my mother to look just as beautiful as me on my wedding day. So I went out and purchased a beautiful white suit trimmed with pearls and a white hat to match. Mom was dressed second best only to the bride! She was absolutely gorgeous! Everyone commented on how stunning Pearl looked at the wedding, and she knew it! One of Pearl's friends asked me, "Where did you get Pearl's outfit?" She couldn't believe that it was Pearl. Mom worked really hard to hold it together in front of family and friends on my wedding day. She was quiet most of the time. Mom carried herself gracefully as the proud mother of the bride from the moment she accompanied me in the limousine. Yes, Pearl rode in the limousine with me because no one in the family thought to step up and bring my mother to the wedding! I made the decision to have her ride with me in the limousine because I didn't want my mom to be a burden on anyone, not even on my wedding day!

When Blake and I went on our honeymoon, Pearl stayed with her oldest brother Patrick and his companion. I was exhausted because immediately after the wedding reception, I had to rush home to pack up my mom's clothes, medication, and food. Whenever Mom did an overnight visit, which wasn't too often, I went through a potpourri of feelings—mainly guilt. If I could have gotten away with bringing my mom along with us on the honeymoon, I would have. I hate asking people for help, and no one thought to extend any assistance, except for Patrick and his companion. I packed everything I thought Pearl would need while I was away. I separated her clothes into bags, put her medicine in a pill box and labeled everything. I had a very difficult time leaving my mother because I knew that meant that her hygiene would be shabby. She needed a lot of directing and prompting that I knew her brother and his companion would not do. I realized that I had to let it go. I found solace in knowing that my mom would be safe and have a great time. Patrick was an accomplished musician and classical singer. Pearl always had a good time whenever she was with her big brother. Patrick would play the keyboard and sing songs to his baby sister. Pearl adored her brother Patrick and his classical singing. Sometimes they would sing duets, and Pearl absolutely loved it.

When we returned home from our honeymoon, we could tell Mom was more confused from the change in her environment. It took her a while to become reacclimated. She washed the dishes over and over, ironed clothes, and repeatedly cleaned the bathroom sink and swept the floor. I didn't fuss with her as much anymore because I learned it was therapeutic for her to perform these tasks. The first night Mom returned home, I tried to strongly encourage her to take a bath, but she refused, so I tried to literally bathe her myself.

During the time my mom lived with us, I struggled to get her to change her clothes on a regular basis. I had to be one step ahead of the game by buying multiple pieces of the same outfits so she wouldn't know the difference. The biggest argument was her wanting to wear boots in the summer time. To maintain my own sanity, I started choosing my battles and letting things go. It wasn't worth the stress! I learned from reading and from observation that Alzheimer's is worse on the caregiver than it is on the patient. After I accepted that, I was able to handle my mother's mental condition better. So I gave up the arguing and let her wear her boots all year long.

Although Mom was a handful, mentally and physically, for Blake and me, she was a big help. Pearl helped out tremendously around the house, and was so appreciative that we took her into our home. However, Mom's condition continued to decline. She started to become combative, and uncooperative at the day care. I had to have meetings with the day care about her behavior. She was trying to tell the day care staff what to do. In my mother's mind, she really thought that she was in charge. I thought to myself, the old adage applies: "What goes around comes back around." When I was a young girl in school, my mom had to go to my school for the same behavior. I felt in some strange way that this was payback. I brought the concerns of my mother's behavior to her doctor. The doctor adjusted her medication, and she became less combative. But then she started trying to cook for us, and we were forced to remove the knobs from the stove.

On Saturday mornings, Blake and I would sleep in late after a long work week. Mom would be fully dressed, seated on the edge of the bed in unseasonal clothes, waiting patiently to go out. Mom went out very often and didn't know how to sit still. On some weekends, she would go to work with me. I would give her pointless tasks to complete just to keep her busy while I worked on something in my office. Occasionally I had to conduct training class. My mom would be in the classroom while I was teaching, as if she were a student. Of course I never called on her for feedback. Surprisingly, students never figured out that the woman sitting in class was the instructor's mom. Mom acted as if she had everything under control and sat there flipping through the binder as if she were following along in the class.

My mother's sleeping pattern had started to change because of the Alzheimer's. It was very rare that she slept soundly throughout the night or for long periods of time. My mother enjoyed going to the mall, so I would take her when I could on the weekends. My mom enjoyed going to the dollar store to buy cups. At one point, cups started to take over our kitchen. I refused to get upset because I realized buying cups made her happy. So I would throw some of the cups away and let her start collecting them all over again. As time went on, it became more and more difficult for me to manage caring for her. She started to hoard food, clothes, shoes and various objects. She would hide objects underneath her pillow, bed and closet. She had several bags and pillowcases filled with shoes, papers, clothes, food and other bizarre items.

When we would go out for dinner, Pearl would bring plastic bags from the house and discretely fill them with food from her plate. My prayers became more intense because I saw the changes in her and didn't want anything serious to happen. I knew my mom needed divine intervention. I had premonitions of her leaving the house in the middle of the night, climbing out of the window, or figuring out another way to turn on the stove and burn down the house. I also had thoughts about my mom committing suicide because of her depression. Mom was very independent all of her life, and it was killing her that she was no longer in control. History started to repeat itself. I was always worried about my mom the way she used to be worried about her mom.

One day I awakened to my mother crying hysterically on her bed. When I asked her what was wrong, she replied, "Maudie just passed away." Mom was crying as if Maudie literally had just passed. The reality was Maudie had passed away over thirty years earlier. But in my mom's mind, it had just happened. I realized that this was a symptom of the Alzheimer's too. Her short-term memory was overlapping with her long-term memory. This was very awkward for me, and I probably wasn't as sensitive as I should have been. I told my mom that Maudie had been dead for over thirty years and that she was resting in peace. Thank God the meltdown didn't last too long.

I reflected on all the horrific stories my mom shared about her mother, who suffered with senility, and began to experience some anxiety about my mom. I was afraid of her dying in the house because she had diabetes and high cholesterol. Sometimes she would steal food from the day care, and we had to keep a close eye on her in the house and at the store. We were afraid that she would sneak foods that she shouldn't have. The excessive stress wasn't good for me because I was expecting my first child. I never wanted any kids because I was mentally and physically exhausted from family drama. With my demanding career, I didn't think I could balance being a parent and a professional. However, by taking care of my mother, I found the confidence to have a child. As my mother's caregiver, I learned sometimes you have to do things as a parent you may not want to. During the Easter holiday, my mom wanted me to take a picture with her and the Easter bunny. It was very awkward for me but I did it anyway.

CHAPTER 11

A Dirty Player

As time went on, it was very tough for me to get a good night's rest. I started checking on my mother in the middle of the night. I began to pray and ask God for guidance because the last thing I wanted was for a tragedy to happen. After approximately two years, my mother's refusal to eat and bathe escalated, and her depression appeared to be getting worse. Her mental condition continued to decline, and eventually when Mom was having a good day, she told me that she knew that I had done the best I could, and not to feel bad if I had to place her in a nursing home. She acknowledged the fact that I was expecting a baby, and told me that if I couldn't handle it, that she understood. Mom knew that the only help I had was Blake. I couldn't believe it! I had been praying, asking God for guidance, and my mom confirmed what I had been praying about. To God Be the glory! That was the confirmation I needed to start exploring placement options for my mom.

We looked for a nursing home for approximately six months before we came to an amicable decision. Although I knew I had to find placement for my mom, I wanted it to be a place we agreed upon. My mother and I visited several nursing homes, and the one we selected wasn't far from my house. I was hoping the nursing home would be close so I could visit her on a regular basis. Mom was placed in Green Acres Nursing Home on Good Friday. Her roommate was a young white lady who was paralyzed and a huge Elvis Presley fan. Mom and her roommate became the best of friends and looked after each other. My mother had the legs to go get whatever they needed, and Amy had the mental capacity for the both of them. Mom continued to attend the adult day care one day a week. This is very unusual for patients who reside in a nursing home. The day care is typically for patients who live at home with their families. However, I wanted Mom to get out on a regular basis just in case I was unable to take her out because I was moving along in my pregnancy. The nursing home was against my mom attending the adult day care but abided by our wishes.

One day the nursing home called and stated that Pearl was missing and never made it home from the day care. I was about to go crazy! My mind started racing. This was my worst fear! Had my father found out where my mother was and killed her? Was she somewhere dead on the side of the road because her blood sugar had dropped too low? My mother hadn't been at the nursing home all that long, so I knew she probably didn't even know the name of the facility even if someone found her. The only saving grace was she was still wearing a medical alert bracelet with my contact information. So I was hopeful. There was a mall close to the nursing home, and I went to check there in the hopes of finding her. I called every establishment in the area that I could think of, asking if someone had seen my mother. Hours later, the nursing home called to inform me that Pearl had been found at an animal shelter across the street from the nursing home. My mom loved dogs and was used to taking care of animals, so the animal shelter was a familiar place to her. The nursing home reported that when the bus driver dropped my mother off, instead of going inside the nursing home, she walked over to the animal shelter. According to the day care, the driver was reportedly distracted because she was on her cell phone. From that moment on, we made the decision that mom would not be returning to the adult day care. They couldn't ensure that she would make it safely back into the building.

Upon my mother's admission to Green Acres, she wasn't placed on the Alzheimer's Unit. The nursing home wanted to give her a chance before placing her on the most restricted unit. However, after that incident, she was immediately moved. This caused her to lose a lot of privileges. Blake and I had avoided this for as long as we possibly could, but it was the best option for Mom's safety. This meant that she would be on a locked unit with older residents, and she would lose a lot of freedom that she previously had. She would also have a different roommate. My mother hated being on the Alzheimer's/Dementia Unit, but eventually she got used to it and started to help out the elderly patients. One time I brought my first born child to visit my mother. While we were sitting in the dining room, an elderly Caucasian resident said to me,

"Give me my colored baby," ironically in a very loving voice. Most people would have been offended by this statement, but this resident was sincere and somehow connected with my baby. So I brought the baby closer for Ms. Nancy to see my oldest daughter. Ms. Nancy was approximately ninety-five years old. She had wrinkles in her skin and long, stringy, gray hair. I was afraid that my daughter Alexis would be afraid of Ms. Nancy, but she smiled as the woman talked to her in a soft and loving baby voice.

I visited with mom at the nursing home on a regular basis and attended all of her staffings and special events. I knew how important it was for the nursing home to be aware that my mom had family. That could make a difference in her care. I knew from experience that residents could get overlooked if families weren't involved. At the staffings, the nurses discussed that Pearl was sometimes non-compliant with showering, eating, and taking medication. The Green Acres staff reported that Pearl could be combative and would sometimes take other residents' belongings. I didn't believe it! I bought my mom everything she needed. She didn't have a reason to steal anything from anybody! I was very upset with the nursing home staff. I started taking it personally and felt like they didn't like my mother and wanted her discharged. Mom was constantly complaining about someone taking her belongings, including her wig! Yes! One day her wig went missing. Little did I know my mom had started misplacing and hiding her own wig.

One day when I came for a visit, I observed my mom's head peeking out from another resident's door. As I stepped off the elevator, I observed her from a distance. She looked to the left and then to the right and dashed into another patient's room. Pearl was cold busted! She came out of the room with the patient's clothes. When I walked up and confronted her, she denied everything I had witnessed with my own very eyes. At that point, I started to accept the inevitable. I was losing my hero to a dirty player by the name of Alzheimer's.

CHAPTER 12

The Dark Days

I believe Mom was entering into Stage 6 of Alzheimer's. This is where caregivers may notice a severe cognitive decline, but the stages can also overlap. Sometimes Mom had a body odor because she totally refused showers and assistance with active daily living skills. Her toileting accidents became more and more frequent, so she had to wear Depends on a regular basis. Mom was confused about the location of her room and started to forget certain family members and her own personal history. However, she always remembered me and the fact that she use to be married to a man name Jesse who she did not like.

I became very concerned because Mom didn't mind people seeing her without her wig. This was very unusual because my mother was prideful and private. My mother was completely bald due to an accident that occurred years ago. Kids were playing outside with the fire hydrant while she was in the process of perming her hair. Mom couldn't get any water and her hair burned out, which damaged the cells that promote hair growth. There was no way Mom would let anyone see her without a wig if she was in her right mind. This only confirmed that my mom's condition had greatly depreciated. Now I was forced to deal with reality. I continued to visit on a regular basis at Green Acres and participate in her staffing and activities.

One day the nursing home called to inform me that Mom was having episodes of falling and they didn't know why. They had an appointment scheduled for her with the neurologist at the local hospital. I took off a half day from work so I could accompany my mom to the doctor's appointment. The nursing home was happy because they didn't have to provide a staff member. My mother had a CT scan of her brain, and immediately following the appointment, she had to go to a neurologist to have the results interpreted. The neurologist was very cold and lacked bedside manners. He was pessimistic about her condition. The doctor stated that my mother had fluid on her brain and was not a good candidate for a shunt or surgery because of her age and mental condition. He was very curious about whether she had ever had any trauma to her head. I was unaware of any trauma, unless she hit her head in the nursing home and they didn't report it. It was a mystery how Mom developed fluid on the brain. I left the appointment feeling hopeless and disgusted. I waited with my mom until the nursing home transportation picked her up. As I watched the gray van drive away, I burst into tears. The neurologist made me feel as if my mother were about to die. I started to think about my mom not being here. I got so depressed that I was unable to go to work after the appointment.

A few months after my mom's appointment, I started to receive an increase in phone calls from the nursing home reporting Pearl had fallen. She was refusing to eat at all three meal times. In the back of my mind, I wondered if the falls could have caused the development of fluid on the brain. The facility reported either "no noted injury" or "minor injury." I tried not to let my mind go there, but I couldn't help it. At one point Green Acres talked about putting my mom in a wheelchair, but it was hard to make a case because Pearl was very active. A person has to meet a certain criteria in order to use a wheelchair because it can be considered a restriction of their rights. That could put the nursing home in a very negative light. When I visited with Mom, she had an unpleasant body odor. I had to wash her up before I could even take her out. The nursing home staff made attempts to get Mom to wash up, but she wouldn't. Being that I used to work in a residential facility for people with intellectual disabilities, I knew the nursing home staff couldn't make my mom shower or eat. Their only obligation was to put forth an effort and document their attempts. I knew I had a lot more authority as a family member. I was able to say and do things that the nursing home staff couldn't do. If the nursing home said or did some of the things that family members did, they could get in a lot of trouble.

I started to feel as if my mother's life was coming to an end. I would sign her out the nursing home to take her to visit family members. Mom didn't remember many of them anymore, but she was good at faking it. My sister Billie Jean died of a heart attack, and I was afraid to tell her. I thought it would make Pearl's mental condition worse. When I finally told Mom that her daughter had died, she didn't appear shocked. All this time, I had prolonged telling her to avoid her being hurt, but she handled it fine! However, it was hard to gauge if she truly comprehended it because of the Alzheimer's. It's difficult for patients with Alzheimer's to process information.

My mom refusing to eat became a huge concern for the nursing home because of her health. Her sporadic eating interfered with her medication and diabetes. She had to eat before taking her medications. They offered Ensure as a dietary meal supplement, but she often refused. The nursing home informed me that they were running out of options. I was very realistic because I knew all too well about staff and patient ratios. I knew the nursing home had limited funding and resources. So I started to go to the facility on my lunch break to feed my mom. Every day it became more and more challenging. I tried talking to her and explaining the negative consequences of her not eating, but it didn't do any good. Her mental condition was beyond logical reasoning. Sometimes I would go back in the evening with my daughter. Alexis, my daughter, sat in the stroller as I fed my mom. I would tell my mom, "You need to eat so you can set a good example for your grandbaby." But it didn't work.

One day while I was out of town, Blake went to the nursing home to feed Pearl. Blake told me, "While I was sitting in the dining room area with Mom, all she did was play in her food. When I tried to convince her to eat, she threw her wig off her head and put her head on the table." He had to help her put her wig back on. Everyone in the dining room just stared. My husband said he felt like crawling underneath a rock. That was too much for Blake, and he never returned to feed her again.

CHAPTER 13

A Dark Christmas Season

The charge nurse informed me that it appeared that my mom's body had started to break down. She explained that when patients refuse to eat, they're usually in Stage 7, which is the very severe cognitive decline stage, the last stage of Alzheimer's. This was hard for me to accept, although I knew it was probably true.

I felt a sense of urgency in my spirit to have my mother renew her vows to the Lord. I felt led to go to the nursing home to pray with my mom. I invited one of my cousins to go with me. We all felt the presence of God in the room. Mom said to me, "I'm tired and ready," alluding to going home to be with the Lord. I had Mom recite a prayer of repentance and salvation to ensure that whenever she made her transition, she would meet the Lord in perfect peace. Mom repeatedly stated, "Yes, Jesus," during the prayer. Deep in my heart, I knew that Mom wasn't going to be around much longer. God had started preparing me for the inevitable.

Shortly after that visit, the nursing home called and stated that Mom was incoherent and that they were rushing her to the hospital. When I arrived, she was still incoherent and unresponsive. While in the hospital, she contracted MRSA (Methicillin Resistant Staphylococcus Aureus); it's a bacterial infection that is resistant to antibiotics and largely acquired in hospitals. I had to put on a face mask, gloves, and a gown before I was permitted to see my mom. I was hurt badly by this necessary safety precaution. I felt like I was visiting a stranger. I had always heard about the infection but couldn't believe that my mom was afflicted with it. How could that be? I was devastated! I was advised not to kiss my mom, which I always did whenever I visited her. I wanted her to feel loved during this critical time.

Mom always knew that I was her daughter, even though sometimes she also looked at me as her mom. I can recall the times when we would be in public and my mother would call me Mom. People used to stare. Tears rolled down my face, as I watched my mother lie in the hospital bed in an unconscious and vegetative state. It was so sad. There were no words to describe the grief I felt as a result of my mother's status. The doctor's prognosis, in layman's terms, was that my mother's body had started to break down from complications of Alzheimer's. It had been seven years since she had been formally diagnosed. Mom had become a hostage to her own body. She also had the triple threat, which was diabetes, high blood pressure, and high cholesterol. The doctor really didn't think Mom was going to recover. She had stopped eating completely. So the doctors had started to prepare us for the worst.

On December 20, 2004, I received devastating news that my mother had less than a week to live due to the fluid on her brain and infections in her body. I immediately called Blake. There was dead silence on the other end of the phone. He was at a loss for words. I had a lot of issues with my family. The split between my parents caused a division amongst us. When I called one sibling, they really didn't say much. There appeared to be an emotional disconnection. One sibling came to the hospital but didn't stay very long. Another sibling came and appeared to be very angry. There was a lot of grumbling amongst family members about me because I took in my mom. Presently, relationships are still awkward with some family members as a result of my decision. I learned that people handle crisis situations differently, but I was mad at my brother and sister for a long time. I felt that they didn't care as much as I did. I had to realize that my faith in God was different than that of my relatives, and I couldn't judge them. God had given me the strength and peace to deal with the situation.

Everything was happening so fast. The hospital placed Mom on hospice. That clearly meant that they were going to make her comfortable as they prepared for her death. I called my husband yelling, screaming, and crying over the phone as I told him the bad news. I went to the hospital the next day and just couldn't stand seeing Mom lying there lifeless and hooked up to machines. The following Wednesday, I didn't have the strength to face my mom again in that condition. I couldn't take it! So I went to the hospital to talk to the nurses and looked at my mom from a distance.

On Thursday morning, the hospice nurse called me to see how I was doing and told me that she had gone to visit my mom. Mrs. Gallagher, the nurse from hospice, said that Pearl was ready to let go, but she needed to know that I would be okay. She said that Pearl's breathing had started to change, and it appeared that she was in distress. She encouraged me to come to the hospital to let my mom know that it was okay for her to let go. Mrs. Gallagher explained to me that my mom could still hear and not to miss the window of opportunity.

When I arrived at the hospital on Thursday, the hospital nurse was there to give me the option of placing my mom on a feeding tube. I started to think about everything my mom told me, and I knew that she wouldn't want to be on a feeding tube. However, the practical side of me felt like if I didn't consent, I would be starving my mother to death. I explained to the nurse that I was in an ethical dilemma. The nurse tried to help me think it through. She explained to me that a person's brain tells them when they are hungry, and she told me Mom wasn't lying there saying to herself that she wanted a cheeseburger. She further explained that my mom's brain was not sending off those types of signals anymore. That made sense to me! There was no significance in placing my mom on a feeding tube because certain parts of her brain were already dead. I contacted my brother and sister to get their input, but really didn't get much feedback to help me make a decision. So I obliged my mother's wishes and refused the feeding tube. I felt in my heart of hearts that she would oppose it.

On December 24, 2004, the very next day, I went back to the hospital to talk to my mom. I cried and told her how much I loved her and how grateful I was to have her as a mother. I thanked her for every opportunity that she had given me. I struggled with telling her that it was okay for her to let go. My mom laid there unresponsive, but I believed in my heart that she could hear me. She looked so peaceful. I was so happy that my mother knew who I was up until the day she became unconscious. She always recognized me by name.

The morning of December 25, 2004, I was on the floor opening up Christmas gifts with my eighteen-month-old daughter, Alexis. I felt it in my spirit that at any moment I could get a phone call from the hospital. I had butterflies in my stomach. I was trying to be happy for my daughter, but I was on high alert for devastating news. The Christmas tree was overflowing with gifts just as it was when I was a young child. However, I didn't feel that we would get through opening up all of the gifts. At approximately 7:00 a.m., the phone rang, and I knew immediately it had to be the hospital. Who would be calling on Christmas morning before 8:00 a.m.? My caller ID started announcing each digit of the phone number. It was the hospital, and I didn't want to answer the phone. When I answered, the hospital representative on the other end of the line stated that Pearl was having trouble breathing and that I should get to the hospital immediately. I threw on my clothes and drove to the hospital by myself. Blake stayed at home with our child. As much as I didn't want to face this by myself, I had no one to call on in my family for support.

It seemed like it was taking the traffic lights forever to change to green. Normally it would take me about ten to fifteen minutes to get to the hospital, but it felt like it took me thirty minutes on Christmas morning. I knew in my spirit that my mother had already made her transition and was at peace with God. When I arrived to her floor, I could see medical professionals going in and out of my mother's room. As I walked up to the door, they told me that I had made it just in time. I wasn't buying it! I knew my mom was gone. The hospital staff instructed me to put on the face mask, gloves, and gown because of the MRSA. The nurse said, "She's struggling. These may be her last breaths." I observed from the doorway. The medical professionals were standing around Pearl's bed, as if they were going to restage their act of saving her. I told them that I knew my mother was gone and they didn't have to do a reenactment for me. The medical professionals looked perplexed at my response. I took off running down the hall screaming.

I called my husband, sister, and brother to tell them the bad news. I was angry! On top of it, I was all by myself. The chaplain arrived and took me to a quiet room to calm me down. He let me rant and rave and release all of my emotions that I had bottled up for so long. The chaplain was very supportive and even prayed with me. When the hospice nurse arrived, the chaplain dismissed himself. The hospice nurse listened and consoled me. She strongly recommended that I seek counseling to prevent me from going into a deep depression. Ms. Gallagher reminded me that I had a husband and an eighteen-month-old baby at home who needed me at my best. For so many years, I felt that I had the world on my shoulders dealing with my family. I lost so many relationships with the split between my mom and dad. When my mother passed away, I grieved for three losses at once. Pearl was my mother, my best friend, and like my child. I looked after her and protected her as a mother would. The grieving process is very complicated, and all of those relationships had to be addressed in counseling.

My mother died one day before her seventieth birthday. She was born on December 26, 1934. This made it bittersweet. Mom had to be a special lady to die on Christ's birthday— and she was! My mother was a saint sent from heaven! I went to make all of my mom's arrangements and invited Valerie to go along with me. I spared no expense for her funeral. She was buried in an elegant white suit inside of an ivory-colored casket close to my home. My father was informed about her home-going service but chose not to attend. He was still angry after all those years. He was mad that she had finally left him and he didn't have access to her income. Jesse often shared with other family members that Pearl ruined things for him. Jesse stated "in this stage of my life I was supposed to be pulling a red bow off of my brand-new Lincoln."

I learned through the funeral arrangement process how insensitive people could be. When I went to sign the paperwork at the funeral home and asked if I could see my mom, the worker told me, "Your mom is upstairs lying on a gurney with a sheet over her body and a pillow over her head." That was literally too much information. This is an image that is etched in my mind. When I went to the cemetery, the person assisting me showed me her favorite headstone. This was very creepy because the headstone had the lady's name on it, date of birth, a dash, and a question mark for the year of her death. I was looking at a headstone with her information on it while she was talking to me. People in this business don't realize how the things they do and/or say can really affect someone emotionally and leave them scarred for life.

On the day of my mom's home-going, I was refusing to go because I couldn't handle it. Somehow in my grieving and distorted mind, I believed that if I didn't go then it wouldn't be true. Blake waited until the very last moment with me, but he had to leave because he was officiating the service. I was able to catch a ride with a friend who was running late for the service. She was so kind to pick me up. I borrowed my friend's sunglasses and pressed on.

When I arrived at the services, the wake was over and the home-going was just starting. I was so broken up that I cried throughout the entire service. My God brother, Byron sat next to me to help me hold it together. That was only the beginning of a long road of counseling to come. My emotions were all over the place. I started to question if I did the right thing by taking my mom in because it caused such a rift in the family. Relatives felt that they had to choose sides. God confirmed every time that I had done the right thing. The truth of the matter is, Jesse had a very bad temper, and he had several guns in his possession. A bad temper and guns do not mix. He could have killed my mother in rage. The decision of what to do with my mom was actually made for me. I had no idea that day I picked my mom up from the house it would turn into a permanent situation.

Going to counseling was one of the best things I could have ever done. The counselor helped me work through my grief in the natural world, and God restored me in the spirit. I had to work through all three losses in order to be made whole again. I was raised to believe that all you need is prayer. God is the counselor. Somehow religious people believe that if you go to counseling, you don't trust in God. However, therapists are clinically trained to help individuals deal with the grieving process. Therapy is another form of medicine. The same way God can heal us through prescriptive medication, he can heal us through counseling and therapy. God has allowed doctors and therapists to be on this earth for a reason. Counseling by a human professional was the impetus in helping me to be restored. I felt that it revealed what I needed to pray for, and I prayed without ceasing! Prayer helped me tremendously with the healing process, and that process was very insightful. I went to a spiritual counselor, which was also very helpful. The counselor used the word of God to help guide me through the sessions. Every session started off with prayer. I discovered that my parents' dysfunctional relationship had a huge impact on me.

I was holding a lot of resentment and anger toward various family members for years for not helping me. I had to learn to stop putting expectations on other people. Don't expect from others to do the same thing that you would. I had to learn to put everything in the proper perspective. It wasn't easy because being mad at someone doesn't require you to make any changes or do any work. Forgiveness requires change and work. I had to learn to forgive, which is something I still struggle with. However, I knew if I wanted to be blessed and be used by God, I had to forgive. So I started my prayers with "Lord, please help me learn how to forgive."

There is not a day that goes by that I don't think about my hero. I knew my mom was going to die, but I wasn't ready. I felt I needed more time. The therapist asked the question, "If you could have more time with your mom, how much time would you need?" I got very angry because I couldn't answer the question. Simply put, it's a question that can't be answered. No matter when a loved one dies, you always feel as if you need more time with them. How can you put a number to how long you want them here with you on earth? The question and the fact that I didn't have an answer helped me to come to grips with my reality. One hundred years still wouldn't be enough. The time is never enough!

Finally, I am in a place where I can smile and say, "Thank you, Lord!" I had thirty-three years on earth with my mom. The holiday season is always tough, and Christmas will never be the same. My mother loved the holidays! It's no surprise that she would be worthy of dying on Christ's birthday. However, one of the best gifts that God ever gave me was the world's greatest mom! For years I couldn't understand why the Lord would take her on Christmas Day. But as time went on, I realized that it wasn't for me to understand. That's why he's God! If we understood God's will, then we wouldn't need God. I eventually accepted the fact that God wanted "his rose" on Christmas Day. When I learned to accept God's will and not question God, I received strength and was delivered from my grief. To God Be the glory for everything he has done!

BIBLIOGRAPHY

Http:<u>www.alz.org</u>

The information used to identify the characteristics associated with the stages of Alzheimer's was obtained by the Alzheimer's Association.

ABOUT THE AUTHOR

Patricia Madina McClure is the author of *Losing a Hero to Alzheimer's: The Story of Pearl*. She has been in the health care industry for over twenty years. Her educational accomplishments include a Bachelor of Arts Degree in Psychology, a Master's Degree in Business Administration and a Master's in Public Administration with a concentration in Health Care Administration. Throughout her over twenty-year career, Patricia has worked with people with intellectual disabilities and mental illness, as well as the geriatric population. Currently, she works as an executive team member at a facility that is owned by a Fortune 500 company; it is one of the largest health care corporations in the world. Patricia also serves as an adjunct college professor where she teaches health care and human resource management courses. Patricia is a member of Alpha Kappa Alpha Sorority Inc. Her love for writing began at an early age. At thirteen, she submitted her first published work to *Ebony Jr. Magazine*. While in elementary and high school, she served on the newspaper committee and wrote various articles. On a college level, Patricia has contributed to a text book in the field of health care.

Patricia is a formal actress in the Chicagoland area, where she studied at John Robert Powers Agency in downtown Chicago. She also attended ETA Creative Arts Foundation, where she continued to hone her artistic skills. Throughout her acting career, she developed her talents through various performances and plays. She continues to use her skills by writing articles for the *Daily Herald Newspaper* to help raise awareness about behavioral health care topics and national initiatives.

Losing a Hero to Alzheimer's: The Story of Pearl was in her spirit for a very long time. However, she needed to be in the right place mentally to write the story about her mom, Ann McClure (aka Pearl). Patricia's mom was her role model and hero, and she shares how difficult it was to see her mom, whom she admired so much, go through the grueling stages of Alzheimer's. After ten years, Patricia felt she was finally ready to share Pearl's story with the world. It is her hope, that anyone who reads this book will be able to identify the stages of Alzheimer's and develop a practical perspective on how to respond to a loved one with the disease. Patricia is a mother, happily married to a pastor, and lives in the Chicagoland area. She is so grateful for the opportunity to be able to encourage someone else that is on the journey of taking care of a loved one with Alzheimer's.

Printed in the United States
By Bookmasters